OUT OF THE SQUARE

Unique Contemporary Residences

OUT OF THE SQUARE

Unique Contemporary Residences

Stephen Crafti

images Publishing

Published in Australia in 2006 by
The Images Publishing Group Pty Ltd
ABN 89 059 734 431
6 Bastow Place, Mulgrave, Victoria, 3170, Australia
Telephone: +61 3 9561 5544 Facsimilie: +61 3 9561 4860
Email: books@images.com.au
Website: www.imagespublishing.com

National Library of Australia
Cataloguing-in-Publication entry:
Crafti, Stephen, 1959- .

Out of the square: unique contemporary residences.

Includes index.
ISBN 1 86470 143 9.

1. Architecture, Domestic. 2. Architecture, Domestic –
Designs and plans. I. Title.

728

Coordinating Editor: Aisha Hasanovic

Designed by The Graphic Image Studio Pty Ltd, Mulgrave, Australia
www.tgis.com.au

Film by Mission Productions Limited, Hong Kong/China

Printing & binding by Pimlico Book International, Hong Kong

IMAGES has included on its website a page for special notices in relation to this
and our other publications.
Please visit: www.imagespublishing.com

contents

introduction

STEPHEN CRAFTI

Brick houses with pitched roofs can be seen in nearly every suburban street in nearly every city in the western world. With their tiled roofs and rectilinear walls, they are indistinguishable from their neighbours and are reproduced en masse. The homes featured in this book challenge the concept of domestic architecture, through the use of unconventional materials and processes. While they may appear irreverent at first, each advances the cause of contemporary architecture, whether in small increments or as larger gestures.

Out of the Square: Unique Contemporary Residences primarily looks at projects that use a variety of materials. Concrete, steel, polycarbonate and timber are reconsidered and translated into designs for the 21st century. One house is completely made of steel. Another house features an unusual steel extension, evocative of a caravan. In yet another instance, a house is fully clad in zinc sheeting. While these materials are not used regularly in domestic architecture, they are proving to be functional alternatives for many architects.

Sometimes, it is the process that steers the architect towards creating something entirely new. The materials aren't always the starting point in a design. One house, called the 'Wrap House', is derived from wrapping the material, rendered-cement sheeting, around the volumes, to create spaces. And while there are identifiable rooms, such as a kitchen, living areas and bedrooms, these areas emerged after the architects manipulated one continuous plane.

Custom-made architect-designed homes don't appear in every street. Like treasures that need to be discovered, they become landmarks in their areas. Sometimes the design speaks loudly to the street, announcing its arrival in the neighbourhood. At other times, the façades are modest and shy away from attention. A Victorian home in the inner city, for example, conceals an extension that bears almost no resemblance to its façade. The addition contains windows and doors, but the roof looks as though it has been carefully folded like origami to maximise sunlight and the surrounding views.

The shape of a great whale is seen in one house. Incorporated into an extension to an existing house, the curvaceous roofline unexpectedly directs the vista towards a garden rather than the ocean. Other designs take their inspiration from buildings nearby. While a block of brutalist-style concrete townhouses built in the 1970s may not be suitable as a large family home, their form and materials are instrumental in shaping the contemporary design of a nearby home.

Another feature that differentiates some of the houses in this book from the mainstream is the unique sites in which they are found. One house, sitting on top of a sand dune, is constructed of steel and painted in striations of green, evocative of the gnarled scrubland. While some houses are camouflaged in their setting, either rural or urban, others create a sharp contrast to their neighbours.

For many owners, developers or investors, architecture is not just an investment. It is way to stimulate the senses. Films inspired some of the designs, while others evolved from childhood memories or holidays spent with family. For the people who live or holiday in these buildings, the varying inspiration for the designs can be fully appreciated on a daily basis. For the readers of this book, I trust their work will also inspire. Each design presented in the book offers something completely new.

A Beacon

ENGELEN MOORE ARCHITECTURE + INTERIOR DESIGN

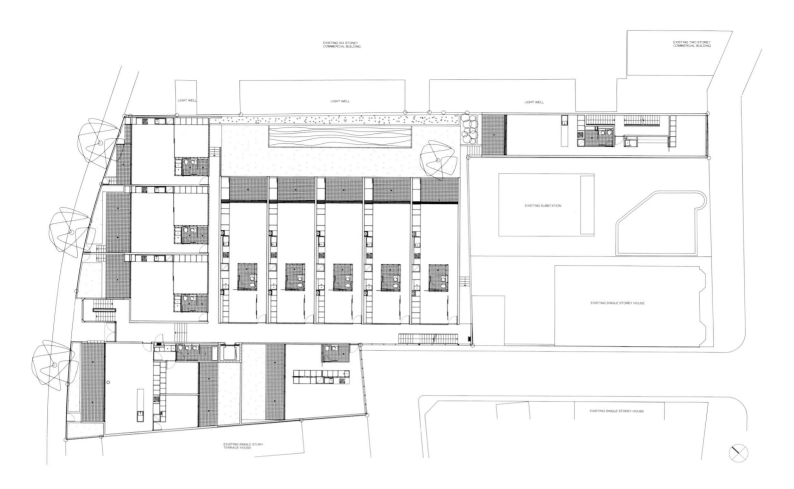

These inner-city apartments were conceived

as a transitional element in the streetscape, between a six-storey commercial building on one side and single-storey terrace houses on the other. The shape of the site dictated that the building be broken down into a number of distinct elements.

Completing the heavily articulated building form is a translucent-white, glass stair tower adjoining the main entry and a three-level walkway giving access to the units. The distinctive 'lantern' at the front of the development also activates the street at night. 'It's a relatively dark street and the lantern also illuminates the school grounds across the road,' says Moore.

There are seven different apartment forms within this 26-unit development, the majority of which contain a 'working wall' running the entire length of the apartment, including the balcony. The 'working wall' contains kitchens, laundries, wardrobes, studies and generous storage areas. This wall is distinguished from the building shell by coloured panels that are expressed externally on the balconies, in contrast to the crisp white concrete structure. Bathrooms, for example, are typically expressed as fluorescent-coloured freestanding pods, placed in the centre of each apartment. They allow breezeways through to the bedrooms, where the use of large sliding panels achieves flexibility between the need for privacy and the free flow of space. Double-height living areas are introduced to upper-level apartments, expressed externally with double-height balconies.

The design of the apartments adopts passive environmental strategies, and they all have excellent cross ventilation. The sliding doors to the balconies slide away into a cavity in the 'working wall' to seamlessly integrate interior and exterior spaces. These apartments don't resemble the usual form that is generally rectilinear and hard up against the street frontage. For Engelen Moore, the development was an opportunity to break down traditional formulas and create something unique.

Photography by Ross Honeysett

A New Model

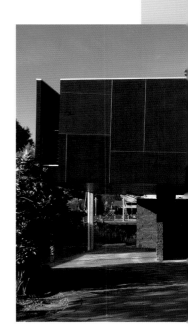

BIRD DE LA COEUR ARCHITECTS

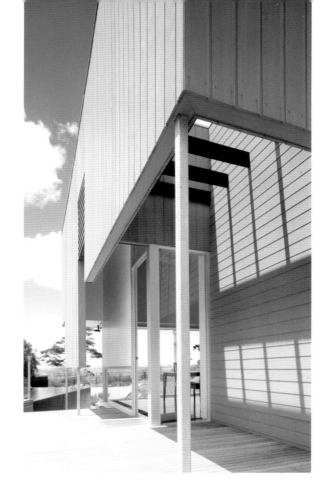

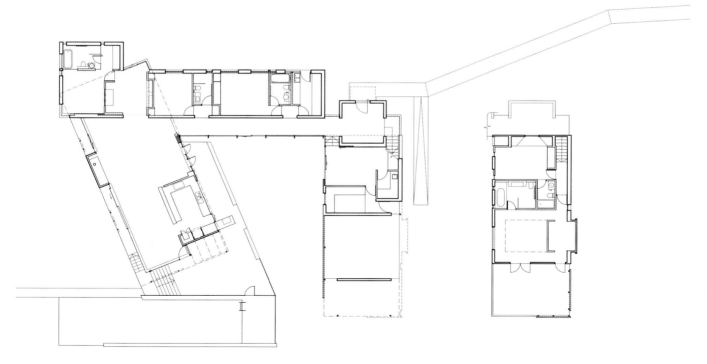

This house was built for an extended family: a mother,

a couple expecting their first child and a sister. But unlike conventional models where there may be a detached flat for the mother, a main house for the family and separate facilities for the sister, the emphasis here is on shared space.

Situated on half a hectare of land, the house is designed around a central courtyard and includes three connecting wings, one of which is a shared kitchen, living and dining area. The pool, angled and elevated to capture the view of the bay, completes the square. "There's a communal aspect to the design without having to queue for a shower," says architect Vanessa Bird, who fondly recalls sharing houses as a student.

The home's façade, made of rough-sawn Ecoply, finely detailed with aluminium, wraps around the elevated front wing that contains the couple's bedroom, ensuite, patio and a separate bedroom for the new baby. The masonry wing includes a bedroom and ensuite for the sister. The mother's bedroom, ensuite and reading room leads from the main kitchen and living area. The spaces are defined by changes in floor level and large sliding doors. A timber and translucent glass Japanese style door for example, screens the mother's wing. "The idea of thresholds was integral to the design," says Bird, who included a number of plinths leading off the main passage to the various abodes. "Even when a door leads off a corridor, it's never direct. You're aware of entering into someone else's space," she adds.

The glazed living wing, which clips over the masonry wing, has spectacular views of the water and neighbouring ridge. It also brings the family together in the most generous space. But from the street, the house appears discreet, simply concealed behind a Mondrian chequerboard façade.

Photography by John Gollings and Emma Nickson

A Sustainable Design

BRENDELAND & KRISTOFFERSEN

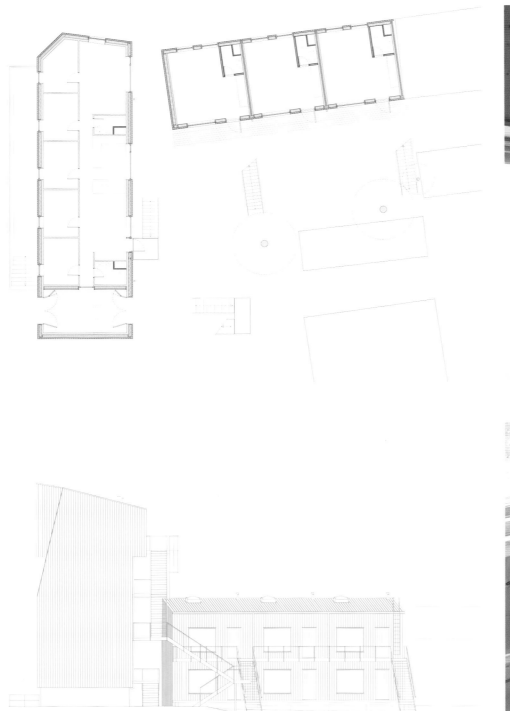

Located in a rather run-down area called

Svartlamoen, these wooden buildings and their adjacent blocks are part of a 19th-century grid – partly residential, partly small-scale industries, with some areas overgrown by weeds and bushes. The project incorporates building strategies closely linked to the unsentimental, functional and surprisingly radical buildings of rural Norway.

All of the structural beams were produced in factories and then assembled on site in the space of ten days. The interior

partitions are 96 milimetres thick. This creates a rough interior where the occupants' furnishings and other equipment can be bolted directly to the walls; additional fine-tuning and customizing of the walls can easily be done with a chain saw or sand paper. This makes for a high grade of flexibility in terms of changes to the program in years to come.

All vertical movement takes place outside the building perimeter, on cantilevered steel stairs. The external stairs are all part of the strategy to limit the overall area of the buildings, and with that, the cost of construction and the need for heating, whereas the wide platforms provide the inexpensive luxury of sunny balconies. One of the objects in the project was sustainability and reduction of energy consumption per person. The outer walls thus have an additional layer of 200 milimetre-mineral wool, gypsum boards and an outer skin in untreated pine.

A Viewing Platform

ENGELEN MOORE   ARCHITECTURE + INTERIOR DESIGN

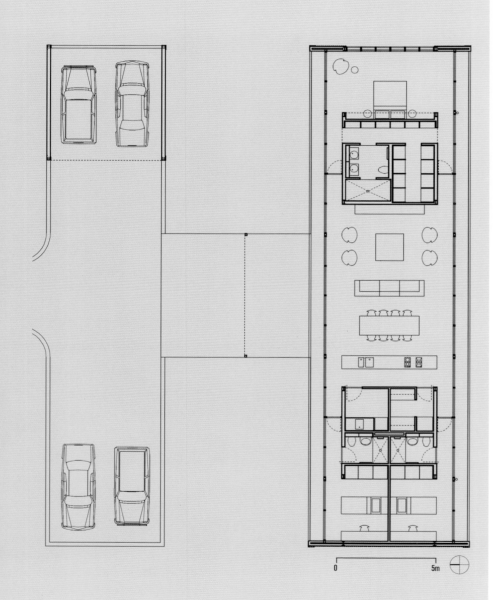

0   5m

This striking house is located approximately

50 metres below the summit of mountain ranges, with significant 180-degree views overlooking the jagged coastline. The architects were keen to use the same language as the rural buildings surrounding the property. Unfortunately, the local authorities had a different view on what constitutes a house (pitched roof and brick walls).

For the clients, a couple with two children, the brief was quite simple. They wanted three bedrooms, with an ensuite attached to each. 'There were few guidelines. But they wanted us to capture the views, which are quite extraordinary,' says architect Ian Moore. 'We really saw the design in terms of a large viewing platform.'

The rectangular plan of this house is divided into three zones, by way of two service cores. The eastern zone is for the parents, the western zone for the children, while in the centre are the kitchen, living and dining areas. By centralising the living areas and pulling the service cores back from the glazed walls, there are significant diagonal vistas in all directions. There is an open platform with an aluminium louvred roof adjacent to the living areas, forming

Photography by Ross Honeysett

the entry to the house as well as a shaded verandah. There are also wide decks running the length of the house on both sides. When the doors are open the entire living area becomes an open verandah space, with exceptional cross ventilation.

In order to minimise the impact of the building on the site, a lightweight steel structure has been adopted. This structure, approximately 28 metres by 8 metres, is cantilevered above two concrete boxes, appearing weightless. The roof is angled to allow for full penetration of winter sunlight, as the weather can get quite cold.

Ambiguous Design

FERGUS SCOTT ARCHITECTS

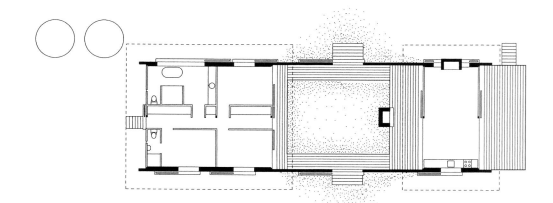

This weekender is located in a relatively

isolated area of the coast. While the beach is only 500 metres away, low swampland makes it easier to jump into the four-wheel drive than walk. A dirt track leads directly to the estuary.

The rural property has been in the same family for years. The client's mother used to take cattle across the property with her father. And while the family moved away from cattle, there are still remnants from earlier days. Some of the temporary structures used by drovers had been blown away

(the winds in the area can be severe). But, before the new home was built there was still a batten and boarded hut on the property, used by the extended family on holidays. 'My client wanted a new house that evoked memories of camping, one step away from being outside,' says Scott

Made of concrete block walls and hardwood cladding, the house takes the form of two slightly elevated pavilions, with angled cantilevered roofs. In between the two enclosed wings is a lawn area, complete with a freestanding fireplace. 'It's quite an ambiguous room. It's roofless and there are walls/doors that can be retracted depending on the weather,' says Scott.

'My client wanted to be able to spend as much time outside as possible. The sliding doors offer some protection.'

One pavilion consists of three bedrooms and a bathroom, while the other pavilion comprises the kitchen and living area. There is no internal corridor to link the two wings, so the owners experience the elements every morning, even before the day begins. As Scott says, 'From a distance the house doesn't appear to be that different. It's a low-rise building that sits in the landscape. But when you start to use the house, you notice the difference. It's still a house, but you feel as though you're camping'.

Photography by Lee Pearce

Bachelor Pad

FRAME LTD

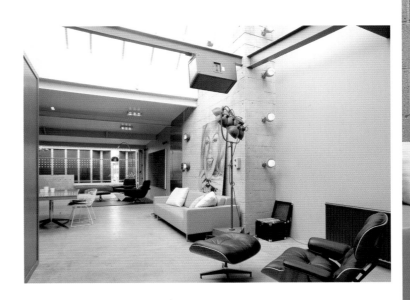

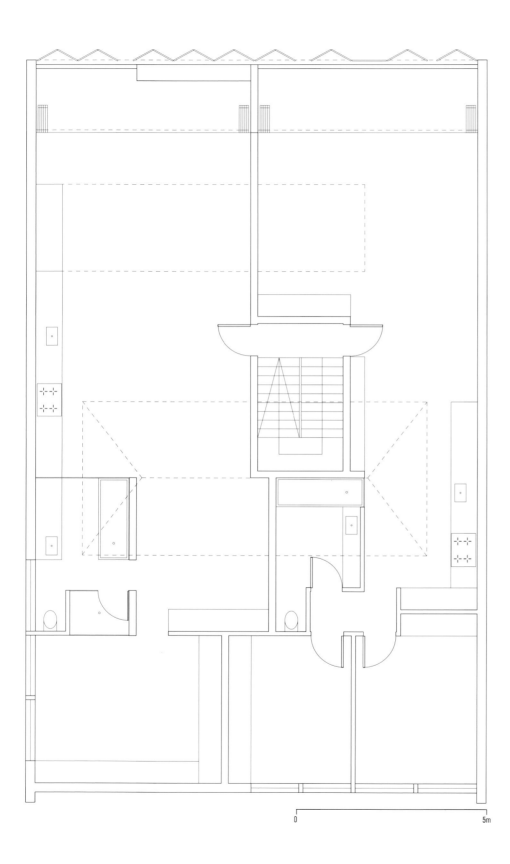

0   5m

Originally an embroidery factory, this inner-

city warehouse has been converted into a bachelor's dream
home. 'My client wanted a sophisticated apartment,' says
architect Andrew Greenslade, who reworked the factory
to include two apartments on the first level and a film
production house, owned by his client, on the ground floor.

As the area is in the centre of the city's red-light district,
security was an issue for the client. 'We wanted to fortify the
design, particularly from the street,' says Greenslade, who
created a strong geometric façade, made of Corten steel panels
and a band in powder-coated steel. In its closed state, the
building is an urban fortress, a feeling that is reinforced by

a concrete wall and heavy Corten steel gates. When open, the screens allow the afternoon sun to enter each of the 180-square-metre apartments, one of which is lived in by Greenslade's client.

While Greenslade reconfigured the spaces, he retained the original glass skylight over the central staircase that links the two levels. The skylight acts as a light well. It draws light into the ground floor, and was one of the key features that attracted the client to this building. It was also an ideal way to combine work with home.

The interior of the apartment has a strong industrial aesthetic, and because the apartment was designed for one person, there are very few divisions. The main separation takes the form of a glazed-wall bathroom, located between the main bedroom on one side of the apartment and the kitchen, living and dining areas on the other side. While clear glass appears on two sides of the central bathroom, the architect also included textured glass to create some privacy. 'It's quite a magical place particularly when the sunshine comes through the skylight,' says Greenslade.

The architect used industrial materials for the interior finishes. The floors are polished concrete and the cabinetry used in the kitchen, living areas and bathroom, is made of oiled steel. 'We also used heavy duty fixtures, many of which were sourced from the city's junkyards,' says Greenslade, whose design has been likened to a gangster's headquarters. 'I presume it will at least keep intruders at bay'.

Photography by Simon Devitt

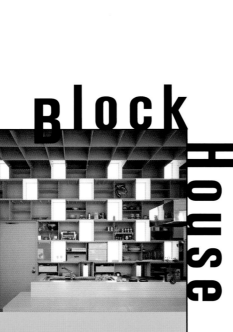

Block House

House

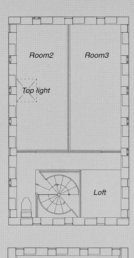

Room2　Room3

Top light

Loft

Void

Top light

Bath room

Terrace

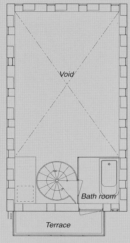

Car

Bed room
1FL-280

Dining · living room

Car

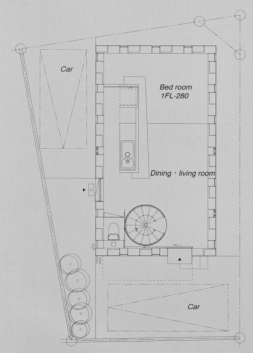

This house was built for a woman in her fifties and her son and daughter. The client who works in the design industry, was also able to offer several suggestions to make living in the house more interesting; for example, the bathroom appears to float, and the washing machine sits halfway up a spiral staircase.

The building is three levels high, with a total area of 32.93 square metres. At first glance the exterior appears like a structure of piled-up concrete blocks, but on closer inspection it can be seen that these are in fact steel boxes. The steel boxes form both the structure of the house and become storage units in the interior. They also work to create a brise-soleil light control, allowing the building to respond to the heat of the environment.

The boxes came in units of five or six and were fused together with high-tension bolts at the construction site. By piling them up in units rather than individually, the architect succeeded in creating a modern design. The boxes were assembled so that they did not fit together perfectly, resulting in lots of openings for light to penetrate the interior, creating a dappled light effect like the sunlight that pours through the leaves in a forest.

Photography by Makoto Yoshida

centred on a Flame

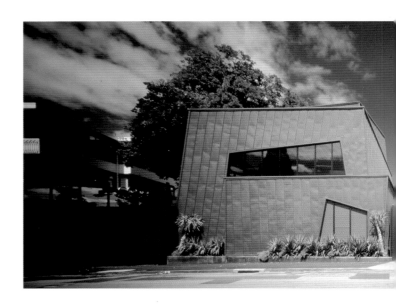

WOOD MARSH ARCHITECTURE

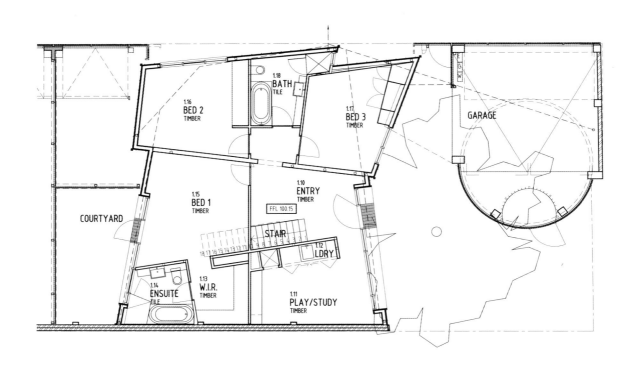

1.16 BED 2 TIMBER

1.18 BATH TILE

1.17 BED 3 TIMBER

GARAGE

COURTYARD

1.15 BED 1 TIMBER

1.10 ENTRY TIMBER

FFL 100.15

STAIR

1.12 LDRY

1.14 ENSUITE TILE

1.13 W.I.R. TIMBER

1.11 PLAY/STUDY TIMBER

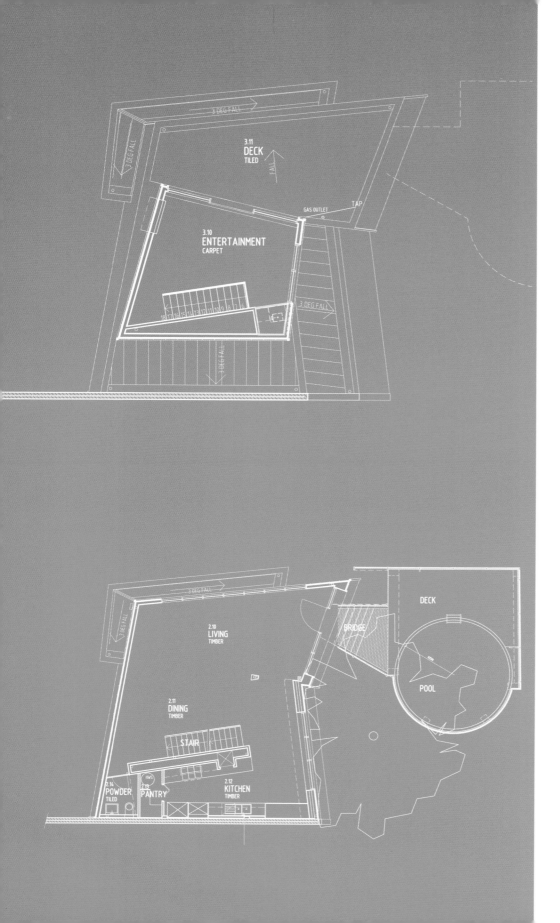

Located on a busy street, this house is

surrounded by walk-up, apartment-style buildings as well as substantial homes. And while there was support from the local council and many neighbours for this contemporary design, there was also opposition from a few local residents. The council now refers to the house as an appropriate response to many inner-urban areas.

The design centred on an established flame tree. The architects accommodated their clients by 'folding' the house, clad in copper, away from the tree. It was a fairly open brief.

Apart from the tree, the clients wanted something that showed a sense of optimism in architecture, something that pushed new boundaries.

Three bedrooms are located on the ground floor, with the kitchen, dining and living areas on the first floor. To maximise the space, Wood Marsh created a curved swimming pool on top of the garage. A deck leads from the study on the second floor. While the design focuses on the courtyard and flame tree, there are also impressive views of the city and the surrounding neighbourhood. Like the form of the house, the windows are irregularly positioned and shaped. 'We wanted to open up the views and create a new perspective on the landscape,' says Wood.

The sense of the garden's dense foliage is drawn into the interior spaces, appearing as an emerald-green tiled column in the living areas. There are also flashes of emerald in the painted feature walls.

While this house is relatively modest in size (approximately 250 square metres), it appears considerably larger and coexists harmoniously with mansions in nearby streets. Volumes are generous and spaces appear to flow endlessly.

Photography by Trevor Mein

concrete

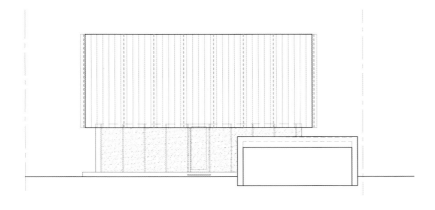

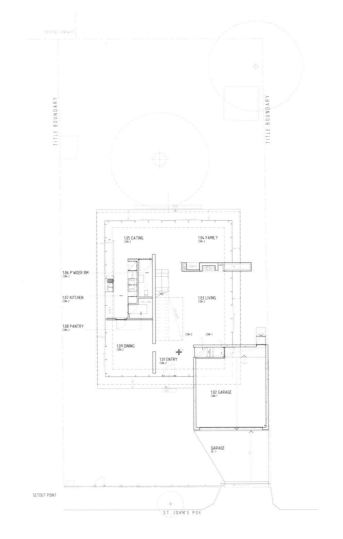

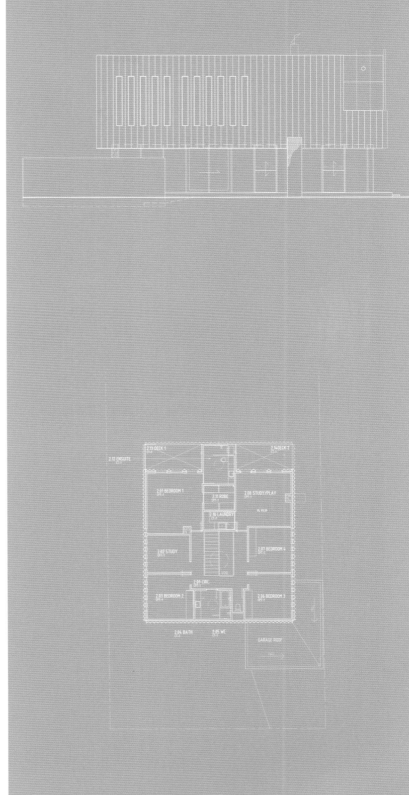

This house, located in a suburban street, is

surrounded by a variety of building types and uses, from Victorian-style cottages to a car yard. Rather than referencing the surrounds, the architects designed a stunning contemporary house.

The brief from the owners, a couple with two children, was not typical of most clients. 'The first word they mentioned was 'concrete', for its aesthetic qualities,' says architect Roger Wood. The two-storey house is set on a concrete plinth that supports glass walls on the ground level, together with a monumental concrete box above. Instead of sharp edges, the concrete form is heavily fluted and appears to hover over its steel-columned base. 'The idea was that it appears to have been carved out of one piece of concrete,' says Wood, who says that neighbours liken the shape to a jelly mould.

Textured glass appears across the front façade (ground floor) to create privacy for the owners. Backlit by green light, the house is activated at night. 'We wanted to give something back to the street. There is that idea of foliage. But it's also about adding colour to a fairly restrained monochromatic palette,' says Wood, who also played down the presence of a front garage by cladding it with timber battens and slipping one corner into the side of the house.

Inside, colour is used sparingly. The primary colour is a scarlet-red tiled feature wall in the main living areas. Set against concrete walls, ceilings and floors, the light reflecting from the tiles adds another texture. The entrance to the dining area on the ground floor is simply framed by an opening made between two concrete walls. On the first floor, accessed by a dramatic steel-and-glass staircase, are four bedrooms and a study. These rooms have full-length glass doors with access to a deck, or narrow slotted windows, 300 millimetres wide and set within the concrete mantel. These windows are almost like tears in the concrete.

Photography by Peter Bennetts

cultivars

JOHN WARDLE ARCHITECTS

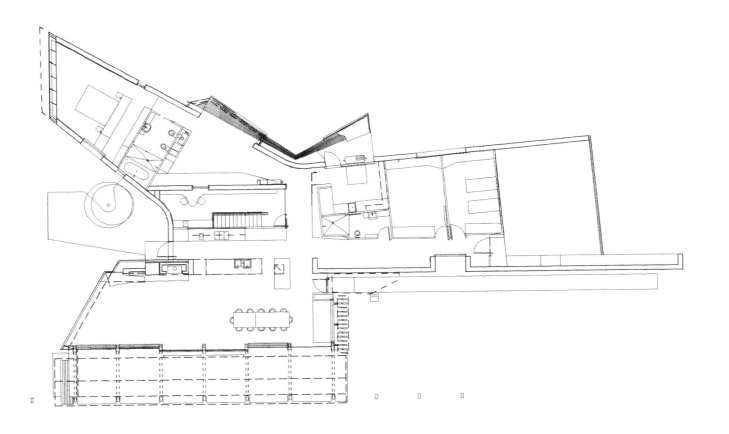

This house came about as the result of a letter.

'It's rare to get a commission this way. It was quite formal, outlining the brief (three bedrooms, living areas etc). But it was important that the design reflected the clients' lives, working closely as they did with the vineyard,' says Wardle. 'The design also had to cater for large groups of people, including wine writers, producers and growers,' he adds.

Before Wardle started to think about the design, he called upon his horticultural training. 'I thought it was important to look at the process of growing the vines, in particular the way "cultivars" (process of grafting) are used to produce the finest crops,' says Wardle, who treated the design of the house in a similar manner. The house has been carefully aligned to the rows of vines, with massive timber posts at the entrance marking out the correlation. In a similar way, the two wings of the house appear to come from a central stem, both simply lopped off at their ends by a pair of secateurs. One stem comprises the main bedroom suite, including the ensuite facilities and a study. The other stem comprises the main living areas. At the centre of the two wings is a large kitchen.

The interior spaces appear to have been drawn out from the rich earth, with walls and ceilings appearing to fold, almost like origami. The main living area, approximately 15 metres by five metres in area, is a grand space and can cater for large groups. During the warmer months, the generous patio is used, allowing for an additional 40 people. 'The design is geared towards their work. Everyone from winegrowers to casual pickers can discuss latest developments in the industry,' says Wardle. The kitchen also caters for larger functions, with a commercial-style central island bench, made of rammed earth and granite. And instead of the usual splashback, Wardle inserted windows that offer unimpeded views of the cool room behind.

The use of rammed earth was included in the clients' brief, and while the architects hadn't used this material before, they were delighted to oblige. It appears in the form of a six-metre-high wall leading to the home. The earth not only evokes the rich soils on the site, but also acts as a canvas for the silhouette of trees near the home. And like the soil, which is considered precious, so is rammed earth. 'We didn't want to build anything into the rammed earth. The steel canopy at the front of the house was designed to drape over the wall,' says Wardle.

Photography by Trevor Mein

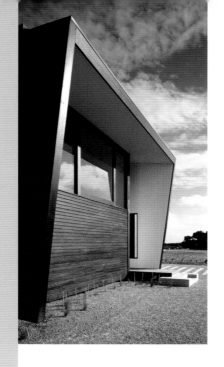

Dune House

JACKSON CLEMENTS BURROWS ARCHITECTS

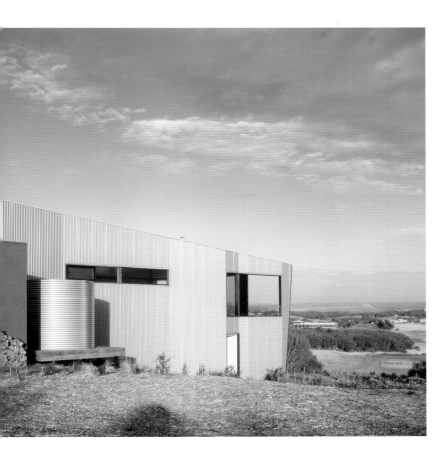

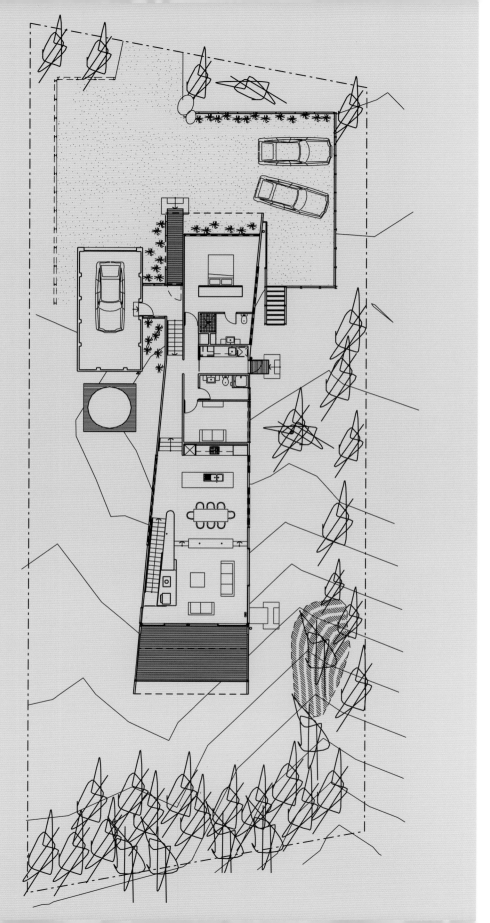

A short distance from the coast, this house

is located on the edge of a golf course on a sand dune that's overgrown with native grasses. In an area with strict guidelines for building, the local authority was keen to avoid pitched roofs and exposed bricks. 'We saw these guidelines as a positive rather than a negative,' says architect Jon Clements.

The architects looked at suitable forms and materials for this site. While the sand dune was relatively stable, imposing a heavy structure above it would have been less than ideal. Light materials were chosen: a timber frame, clad in

Colorbond steel. Three different colours were used to create a series of vertical stripes, one grey and the other two in tones of green. As light crosses the building, the band of colour creates striations across the dunes and over the golf course. The colours also capture the native landscape, with its subtle gradations.

Approximately 100 metres above sea level, this house follows the outline of the dune, appearing to cling to it. But inside the spaces are dispersed over four levels. An entry leads directly from the carport. To one side of the entry, at a slightly higher level, are the main bedroom, ensuite and study. In the other direction, a few steps below are the kitchen and living areas. And on the lowest level, below the main living areas, are two additional bedrooms (for guests) and a separate bathroom. A separate entry to the guest accommodation ensures a certain degree of independence for visitors.

Adjacent to the living areas is a generous terrace, framed with toughened glass and protected by an angled canopy. A timber pergola over the terrace provides sun protection and creates shelter from the prevailing winds. 'It's a fairly robust house. But it's quite an exposed site,' says Clements, who appreciates some of the comments from neighbours. 'Some have said it looks like a military supply shed. In this environment, the idea was to camouflage the house'.

Photography by Shannon McGrath

folded House

DALE JONES-EVANS PTY LTD

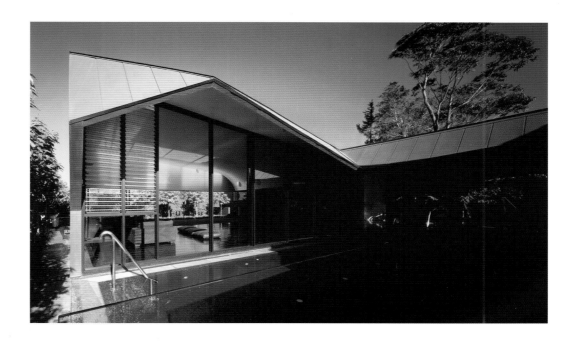

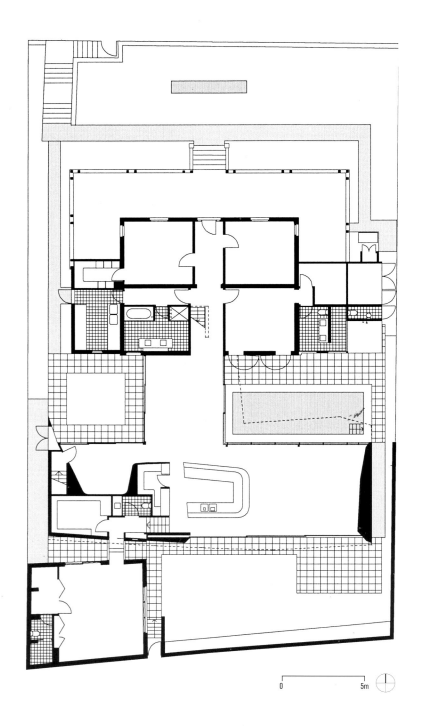

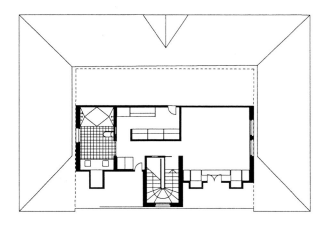

The original house, a Victorian-style home, was extensively
renovated and a new wing, comprising the kitchen and living areas was added.

The core of the house has a folded roof made of copper sheeting. The shape of this roof not only controls the amount of sunlight reaching the interior spaces, but also provides protection for the three external spaces surrounding the new living areas: the pool area, the courtyard and garden terrace. 'The angles of the sun have been worked out to the nth degree. The angles follow the path of the sun, in both and winter and summer,' says Jones-Evans.

Photography by Trevor Mein and Paul Gosney

The origami-like roof also appears magical from inside the house, as it folds to its lowest point over the kitchen and soars above the living areas, framed by floor-to-ceiling glass windows/doors. For the owners, creating transparency in the home was also important. With small children and a pool, there needed to be rigorous surveillance.

The brief was fairly open, with instructions to retain some of the finest elements from the original home. As Jones-Evans says, 'We didn't want to just add a glass box to the original house. The idea was to create something new for how my clients want to live now'.

Glass Lantern

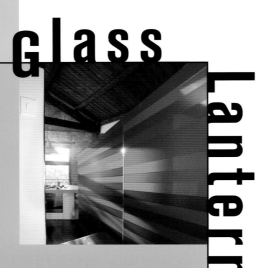

CASSANDRA FAHEY ARCHITECT

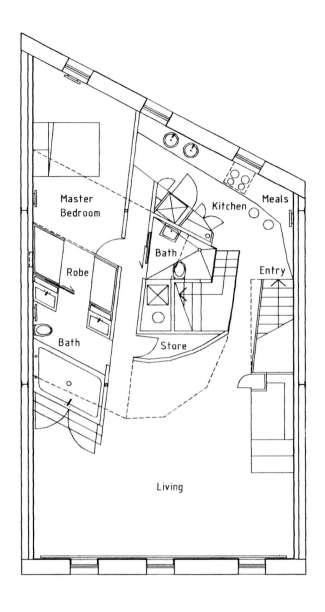

Master
Bedroom

Kitchen

Meals

Bath

Entry

Robe

Bath

Store

Living

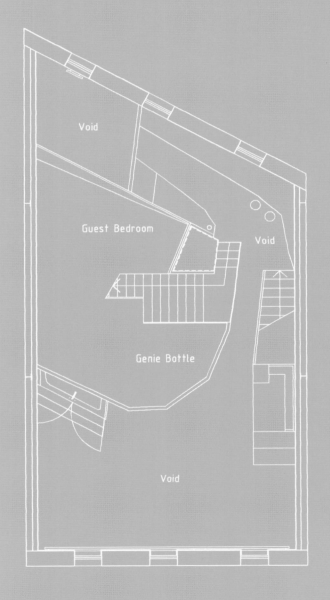

Void

Void

Guest Bedroom

Void

Genie Bottle

Void

This warehouse shares a similar façade to its

neighbours. However, it conceals a dynamic interior that bears little resemblance to a traditional home, though the design includes a kitchen, living areas and bedrooms.

The renovation was designed by architect Cassandra Fahey as her own home, which she shares with her partner Michael Ben-Meir. The building's original trusses, Oregon flooring and timber staircase are the only original features. 'We didn't see the point of obliterating the past. But at the same time, we wanted to create something more challenging,' says Fahey.

The main living area of this home features a large glass tiled 'lantern'. Made up of 450 glass tiles, of varying sizes and five different colours the lantern frames the main bedroom, two bathrooms, a guest bedroom and a mezzanine level. The steel framed lantern not only allows artificial light to filter into the living and kitchen areas, but emits a high degree of luminosity.

Like the lantern, which cuts an impressive swathe into the living space, the main bathroom makes its presence felt, particularly when the screen door is kept open. This bathroom has been entirely custom-made with moulded resin sinks. The second bathroom/powder room features mirrored angled walls.

To divide the architectural practice on the ground level from the living areas above, Fahey inserted a gold-painted timber door midway through the ascent.

Complete with fluorescent-pink acrylic disks, it's referred to by Fahey as the 'cheese grater'. Once past the 'grater', there's a sense of compression. The stairs narrow and the kitchen joinery, featuring digital images of Ben-Meir as a five-year-old child at a birthday party appears. The enlarged images printed on laminated kitchen cupboards are 'reminiscent of lime cordial served in red plastic cups,' says Fahey.

There are a number of large gestures in this warehouse. But for each brave motif, there are several quieter statements, equally as impressive. Mirrors, for example, frame each window to bring in additional light. As Fahey says, 'the warehouse is like a living cell – each cell can expand and contract.'

Photography by John Gollings

Great Whale

IREDALE PEDERSEN HOOK ARCHITECTS

The extension to this house is evocative of a

caravan. 'It could be seen as a caravan. But the design has also been compared to a great whale,' says architect Adrian Iredale. For the owners, who occasionally spot whales from another house further along the coast, the comparisons are well founded. 'The owners didn't have the same views with this house. But they did want us to make a connection to their time spent elsewhere. They also wanted us to achieve a connection with the landscape, even though this house is in the suburbs while the other house is surrounded by rugged coastline'.

The original house on the block, designed in 1925, didn't respond to the suburban site. Like most homes of this era, the focus was internal, rather than towards the garden. However, given the presence of a school over the road and walk-up flats behind, making connections to the garden proved difficult. 'We looked at the project in terms of the house and the garden as one, rather than treating them separately,' says Iredale, who angled the new extension across the rear garden, away from the flats. The elastic plan also follows the path of the sun.

The new wing, comprising 130 square metres, is brick on one side and has a generous glazed curtain wall on the other. Unlike the pitched roofline of the original home, the new roof is made of Zincalume and cleverly wraps around the new form. The end point of the curvaceous roofline doubles as an external seat. In the interior, the same line becomes a shelf in the living area, for television and video equipment.

The new wing comprises a large kitchen, and living and dining areas with the emphasis on the garden. Large glass bi-fold doors open to the timber deck, which can be pulled right back during the warmer months. The organic form has been likened to the architect Alvar Aalto's work. Not surprisingly, Iredale was touring Finland and visited the architect's work shortly before this extension was finished. 'There is that influence. But it was about creating something that celebrated the outdoors, something that was more extraverted than the original home'.

Photography by Robert Frith, Acorn Photo Agency

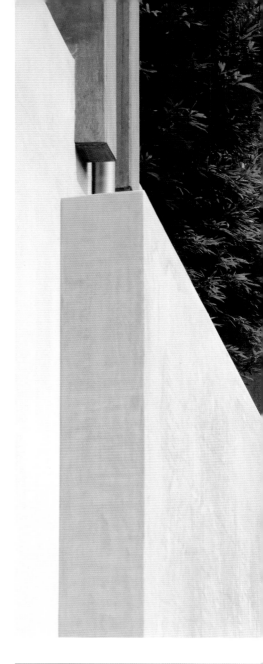

LOW
SLUNG

ALEX POPOV & ASSOCIATES

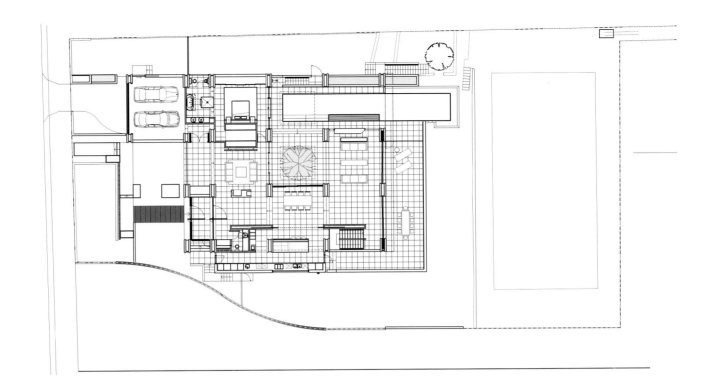

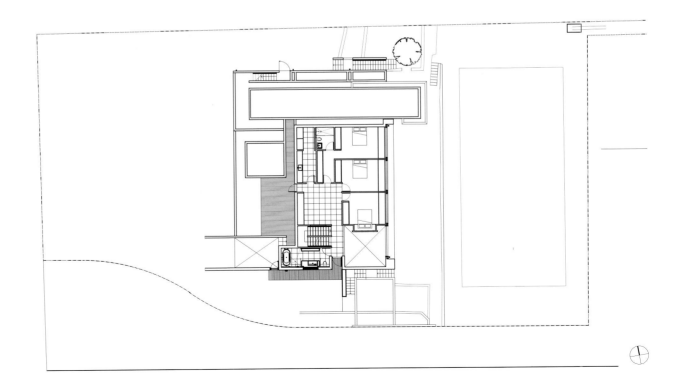

For architect Alex Popov, the opportunity to

design a single-storey home, rather than a multi-storey one, caused an adrenalin rush. 'There's something quite special about a single-storey home. It has quite a gracious feel. It gives you the chance to really explore the site,' says Popov, who subsequently designed all the main living areas on one level, with bedrooms below. The site's unusual 32-metre width allowed Popov to create spacious adjacent rooms to, rather than following a linear path.

The owners had lived in Japan where space is at a premium, so the idea of living with fewer levels had great appeal. The

house also reflects the Japanese aesthetic that is pared back and minimal. Popov designed the house in precast concrete, including 48 precast concrete columns. The only other materials used are steel for the barrel-vaulted roof and timber, both for internal detailing and external awnings such as a screen at the entrance to the house.

Popov used the barrel-vaulted ceilings to define the spaces within the home. Each vault frames a room, whether it's a dining room or living area. One of the vaulted ceilings, above the pool and central courtyard, features generous skylights. 'I wanted to increase the amount of sunlight in the core of the house,' says Popov, who deliberately turned the house away from the street.

Somewhat surprisingly, given the brief, the house is explored through a series of levels. The entrance occupies the lowest part of the house and feels relatively compressed, compared to the living areas. However, as you move through the house, the ceiling heights increase substantially, as do the views over the bay. The living area offers the most spectacular vista, with high ceilings and glazed windows/doors that slide into precast concrete cavity walls.

While there is no sign of the bay from the driveway, a small Japanese-style pond at the entrance to the home sets up the promise of water ahead. Some neighbours have remarked on the home's plain appearance from the street, however, the idea wasn't to announce its arrival to everyone in the neighbourhood.

Photography by Kraig Carlstrom

Luminous Design

KENNEDY NOLAN ARCHITECTS

These inner-city townhouses create a striking

form on their corner site. Surrounded by warehouses, light
industrial buildings and a few Victorian cottages, the
architects were keen to avoid traditional domestic architecture.
'It's quite an ambiguous building. The idea was to respond to
the surrounds. A series of conventional townhouses would
have been inappropriate,' says architect Patrick Kennedy.

The original shell of the 1970's warehouse, once used for
manufacturing clothing, was retained. The brick walls were
finished in 'shot concrete' (for texture) and three, three-
storey townhouses were inserted into the existing shell.
The exterior walls of the townhouses are constructed in
shiplap timber and stained black. 'The timber is quite refined

compared to the rough concrete,' says Kennedy. The other reason for retaining the walls of the original warehouse relates to Council's present setback requirements. 'We knew that if we pulled the building down, we would lose considerable land,' he adds.

The architects were also keen to create a 'mansion' style house typology, rather than three distinct row or terrace houses. 'Rachel (Nolan) and I didn't want the design to appear fragmented. The idea was that it appear as one large building from the street,' says Kennedy.

The three townhouses vary in both size and configuration, ranging from 210 to 250 square metres. All three townhouses are spread over three levels, and feature internal light-wells and exposed concrete-block walls. 'Plaster walls often make a building feel quite light. We wanted a sense of solidity, both inside and outside the building,' says Kennedy. The largest townhouse (located on the corner) includes a bedroom, office bathroom and laundry on the ground floor. The kitchen, living and dining areas, and two bedrooms are on the first level, and two bathrooms are on the second level.

The outdoor spaces take the form of large decks, light-wells featuring strong graphics and in one instance, a courtyard. To create the sense of an outdoor room, Kennedy Nolan included large domestic-style pendant lighting on the balconies. While the vibrant yellow lights make a welcome addition to the street during the day, at night some of the gold-painted interior walls add their own luminosity to the neighbourhood.

Photography by Derek Swallwell

op Art

DURBACH BLOCK ARCHITECTS

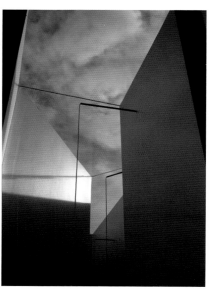

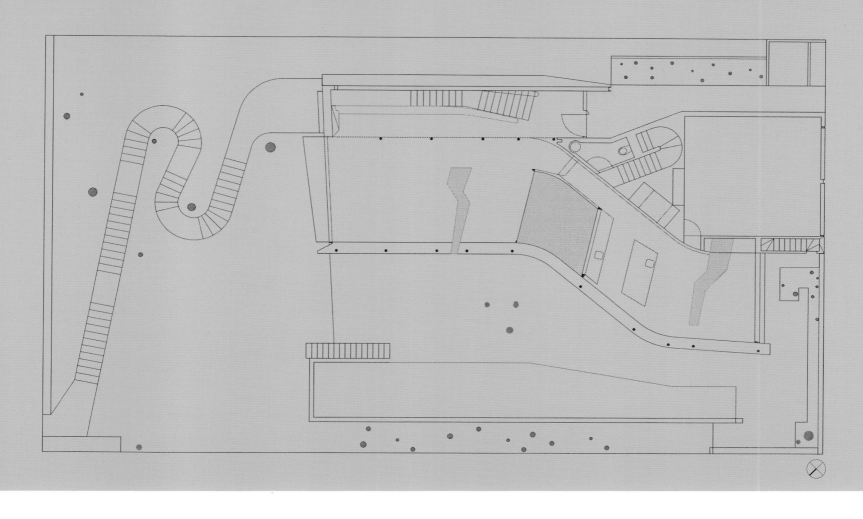

From the street, this harbourside home

appears like a piece of op art. The rectangular façade, made of tilted glass and steel, picks up shadow lines from the sun as they move throughout the day. It also conceals the home's impressive curved side elevation.

For this architectural practice, which has completed several smaller homes in the vicinity, this was an ambitious brief. It included numerous bedrooms, a guest room, study, living areas and pool. And while the site is generous (1000 square metres), the request was for a 500-square-metre house. 'The question was, how do we make a large house appear delicate, not like a bloated mansion?' says Durbach, referring to the trend towards larger homes on smaller sites.

The solution was to create a three-level house that appeared as two. Durbach Block created a large stone podium, with a mantle made of Canadian cedar perched on top. 'The cedar is like a curtain,' says Durbach, referring to the one-inch-wide strips of glass inserted into the timber. 'The slivers allow the light to enter and animate the interior,' he adds.

On the lower level are three bedrooms, a study, laundry, sauna and bathrooms, together with generous storage areas, all accessed via a lower entry point.

On the ground level are the kitchen, living and dining areas, overlooking the swimming pool and harbour. The main bedroom, ensuite and guest bedroom are on the top level.

The home's intriguing interior was achieved by the use of a rich but restricted palette of materials that includes Japanese Sen timber veneer for a number of the walls and Indian slate on the floors. Two voids, which cut through the home's s-shaped elevation, add drama to the spaces as the light changes through the day.

Photography by Anthony Browell

protective Shell

STEVENS LAWSON ARCHITECTS

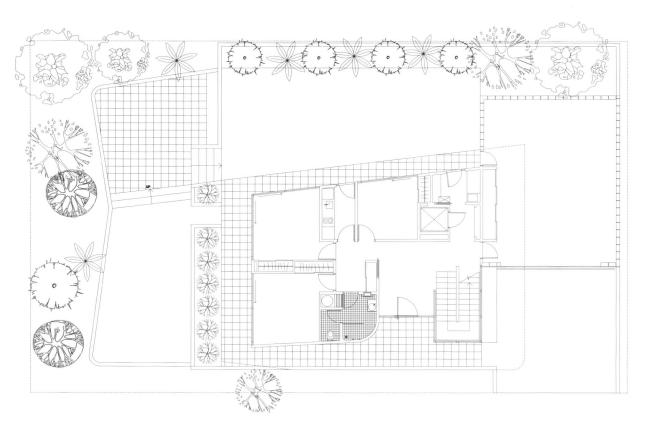

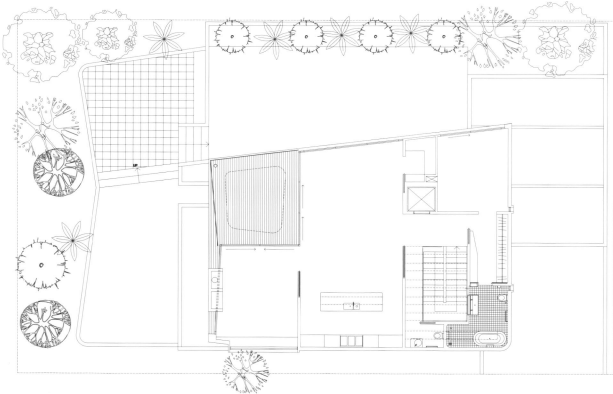

This striking contemporary house has a strong

sense of the past. Not surprisingly, there are two significant
neighbouring buildings: one a modernist 1950's house, the
other a set of brutalist-style concrete townhouses, sculptural
in form. 'We couldn't ignore these significant buildings.
They're as important as the views over the bay,' says architect
Nicholas Stevens.

While the area of the elevated site is relatively modest,
approximately 600 square metres, the architectural gestures
are considerably grander. The two-storey home, designed for
a couple with an older son, goes against conventional design
principles. Instead of bedrooms being located upstairs and

living areas on ground level, leading to the garden, the architects reversed the plan. 'Our clients really thought of this house as a long-term proposition. They wanted a self-contained apartment style home on the top floor and separate accommodation and facilities for their son. They even asked us to include a lift so they would never have to move,' says Lawson.

On the ground floor are three bedrooms, kitchenette, laundry and bathroom facilities, together with parking. The main bedroom, ensuite, living and dining areas, together with a library that leads to a generous patio, are on the first floor. The configuration of rooms is unusual, specific to the clients' requirements.

The materials that have been used for the house make it stand apart in the street. The architects conceived the design in three layers. The first layer is the

textured-concrete retaining wall (insitu-cast concrete with indentations of timber). The ground level, clad in cedar battens and frosted glass, acts as a podium. And the first storey, cantilevered over the ground level, is made of lightweight fibreglass applied with concrete, cast in moulds.

'The house is fairly open, so we wanted to create a protective shell for the more public side of the house and glazed where its private, screened from the street,' says Stevens, who enjoys the juxtaposition of two very different materials. 'It's not usual to have something that appears heavy on top of a more lightweight structure, he adds'.

Photography by Mark Smith

Refined Tin Shed

STUDIO 101 ARCHITECTS

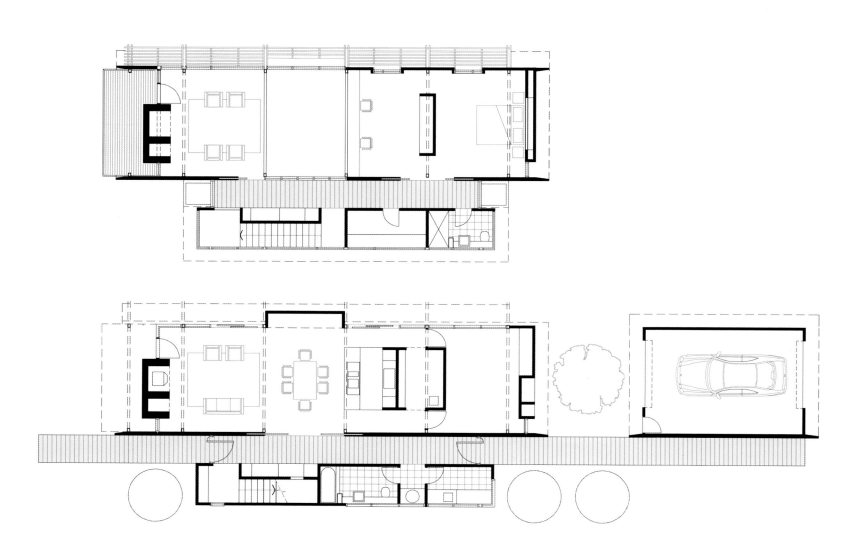

Located on the city fringe, this striking house

is evocative of the farmer-built tin sheds that are dotted throughout the region. It was designed for clients wanting a piece of architecture discreetly incorporated into the environment.

An important element of the design is the butterfly roof, made of Zincalume custom orb. The Zincalume wraps around the house. A large gutter runs down the centre of the house, acting as a collection point for rainwater. Glass, sandstone and plywood were applied to a timber frame. The sandstone used at the front doubles as an internal chimney flue and provides an anchoring element. 'It's like a giant peg. All the other materials used are relatively lightweight,' says architect Peter Woolard.

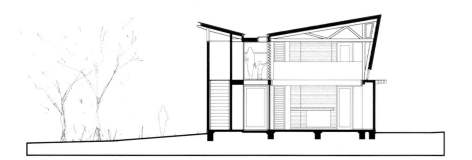

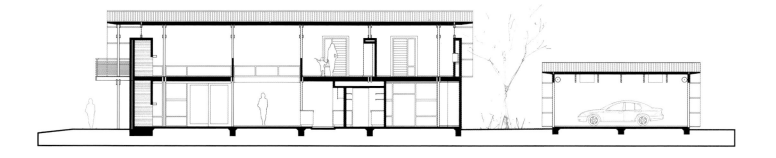

While there isn't a strict entrance, (the back door is often used as it is near the garage), the approach to the house is from a dirt track. Glass pivoting doors at both the entrance and the rear create transparency and the surrounding water tanks provide an alternative to the usual garden features. 'The tanks are a necessity for storing water. But they also act as a buffer for the wind,' says Woolard.

Essentially designed as two pavilions, the house is divided by the bridge or spine. The larger pavilion consists of the main living area on the ground floor, including the front sitting area, the dining area, the kitchen and a multipurpose room. A second sitting area, a study and a main bedroom are located on the first floor.

The secondary pavilion includes a bathroom and laundry on the ground floor. Upstairs, there's a walk-in wardrobe and ensuite. A-floor-to-ceiling glass louvred wall above the dining area links the ground and first floor. 'The bridge is like a breezeway. Light can filter down to the ground floor (through the slatted timber ceiling) and the doors can be left open on warmer days,' says Woolard.

The garage, separated by a courtyard, mimics the shape of the house. Complete with angled Zincalume roof and plywood walls, it also features translucent polycarbonate sheeting to allow filtered light in. Like the garage, the house features some traditional markings (front doors and windows). But from a distance, both forms could be mistaken for farm sheds.

Photography by Trevor Mein

smooth Lines

USHIDA FINDLAY PARTNERSHIP CO LTD

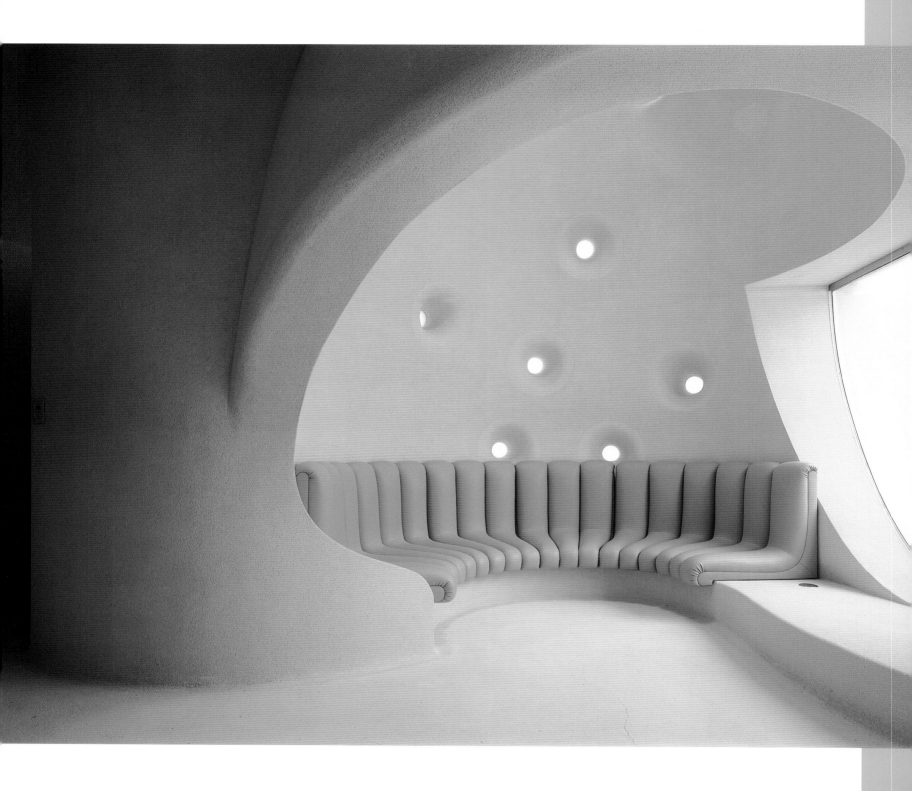

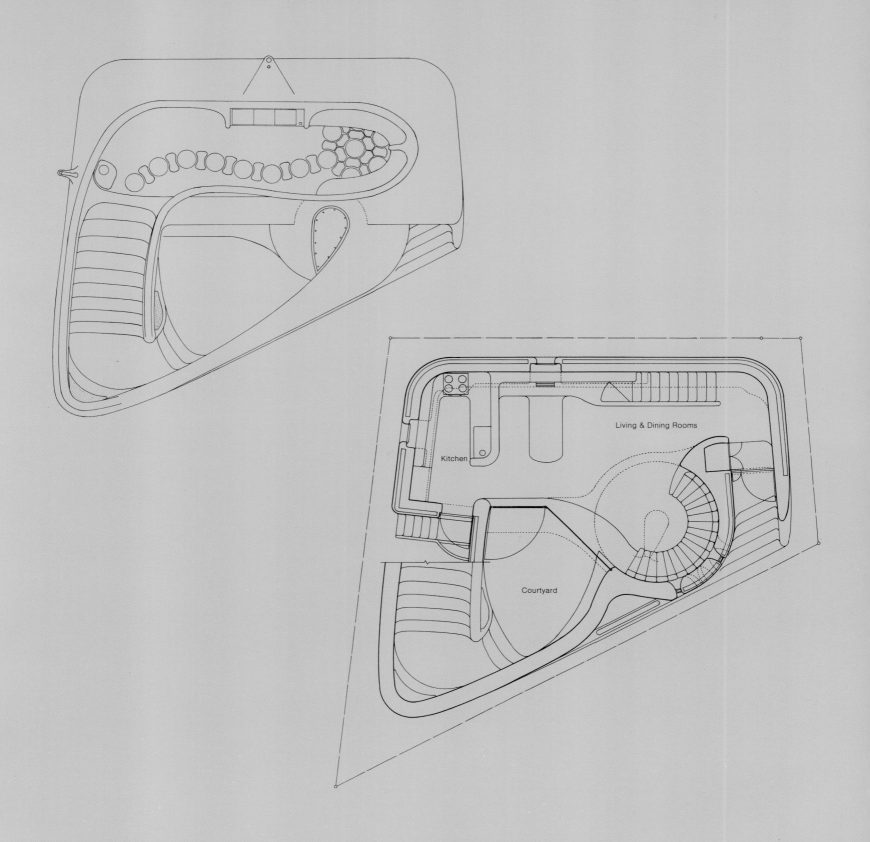

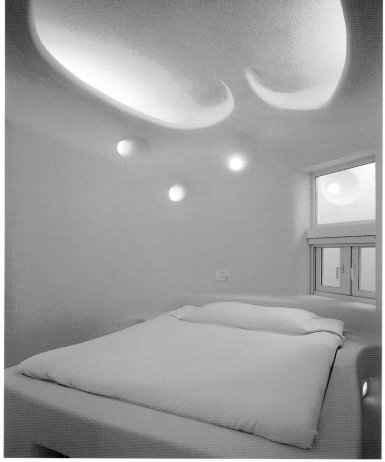

Built using a construction method called the

Truss Wall Method, this private residence uses curved surfaces throughout. The architects sought to create a totally innovative space that gives the impression of physical flexibility and fluidity of a living organism.

A double-wall structure and a roof garden were employed to achieve an ecologically oriented system. The walls and the floors function as a heat storage battery, so that the house maintains a stable temperature. The design also focuses on the topological arrangement of the void (space) and the solid (structure) available in the limited area of the site. The architects wanted to acquire a sense of balance and fluidity and attempted, 'to stuff a series of slimy organs into the limited space.' They also aimed to maximize the horizontal plane, extending it from the living room to the courtyard and up to the roof.

Photography by Tim Griffiths

The architects believe that experiencing such a space would move people deep into their subconscious, stimulating their intuitive sense of space, releasing their primitive desires and liberating their perception. As the architect and environmental artist Frederick Kiesler said, 'Creating a topos pregnant with stimuli that would evoke creativity, will allow for participation in the process of creation, thus making a space which functions as a medium.'

Two Parts House

BLACK KOSLOFF KNOTT ARCHITECTURE

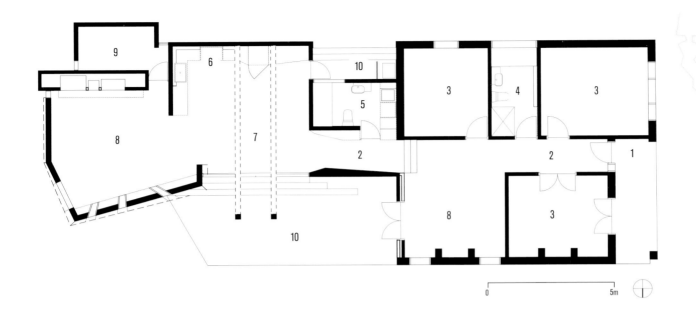

1 Porch
2 Hallway
3 Bedroom
4 Bathroom
5 Bath/laundry
6 Kitchen
7 Dining room
8 Living room
9 Study
10 Deck

0   5m

Originally a Californian Bungalow, this house was almost

demolished before the architects and clients decided to add a bold and contemporary new wing. 'One of the strongest ideas is the radical planning for its day,' says architect Simon Knott. 'The layout of the new wing was loosely inspired by a Victorian love seat, where people sit back to back,' says Knott, referring to the interlocking arrangement of the new kitchen/dining area and library.

Instead of simply adding a glass box, BKK was interested in creating a new form. Constructed of silver ash that has been radially sawn, the new kitchen, dining and library appear to have been compressed. In the library for example, which features built-in bookshelves and elongated windows, the ceiling slopes

significantly. 'The owners are both academics. The idea is that the structure is almost sagging from the weight of the books,' says architect Julian Kosloff. 'The windows have also been designed to catch the angle of the sun at various parts of the day,' he adds.

Inspired by the radical ideas of the Arts & Crafts movement, BKK was also keen to include some new ideas for this extension. While the kitchen is open plan, it also includes moveable joinery. A kitchen table, that appears as a butcher's block can simply be moved around for the owner's convenience. And though only a small detail, the wood box in the living area has been placed vertically into the timber wall, adding texture to the spaces. As Knott says, 'It's that type of detail that attracted our clients to the period home in the first instance'.

Photography by Shannon McGrath

urban

Fortress

WOOD MARSH ARCHITECTURE

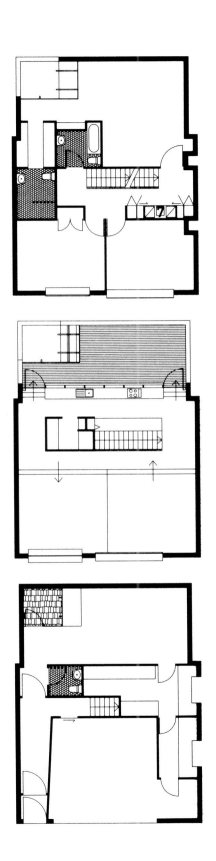

For photographer Andrew Curtis, capturing industrial objects on film is an ongoing obsession. Utility stations, together with overhead wires, are an intriguing part of the urban landscape he photographs. So when it came to looking for a site to build on, this light industrial area seemed ideal.

The house features a separate office and darkroom for Curtis' photography, on the ground floor. Three bedrooms are located on the second level, and the kitchen, dining and living area (with access to a large deck) are located on the top floor.

In order to maximise the site, spaces extend to the boundary, but there was sufficient room to include a small courtyard that provides light and ventilation for the ground floor studio, as well as for the main bedroom.

The frosted-glass doors and perforated-steel staircase that connect the three levels also allow light to enter the inner core. Rather than use traditional handrails for the staircase, a series of balustrade walls (also perforated) create a wonderful dappled light.

The façade, which is made of a variety of grey coloured bricks, takes on a slightly medieval quality together with the building's deep-set windows. While the façade to the street is more fortress-like, the rear façade was conceived like a large painting that simply captures the city views. The architecture of this house illustrates a very conscious notion of texture and the split-concrete walls are a complete break from the usual plaster walls. 'We wanted the design to be fairly bunker-like without it having too much of a presence to the street,' says Curtis.

Photography by Andrew Curtis

winter cocoon

24H ARCHITECTURE

This extension was made to an existing cabin located on a piece of land alongside a waterfall in Sweden. As the site was located in the nature reserve Glaskogen along the lake Övre Gla, there were some building restrictions. 'This was the ultimate opportunity to test the architectural themes of the office,' says the architect.

A proposal was made based on the principle that the extension could be extractable, like a caterpillar. The extension unfurls like a butterfly; during the winter it's a cocoon, compact with a double skin against the cold.

Photography by Christian Richters

During the summer the building can change its form or, like a butterfly, unfold its wings for extra shelter during rainy days.

The extension cantilevers over the waterfall, giving an extra dimension to the house by integrating the natural phenomena of the site. Based on previous experiences the building was detailed using available local building materials. Western red cedar was used for the shingles, which will turn grey with age and make the building blend into the landscape.

wrap
House

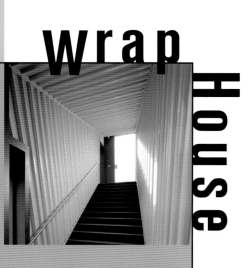

BLACK KOSLOFF KNOTT ARCHITECTURE

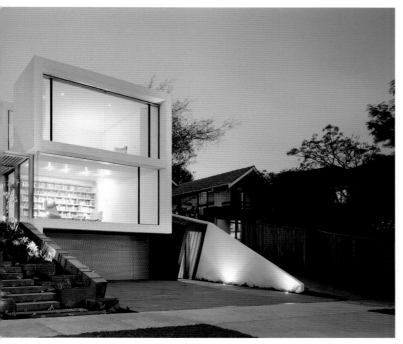

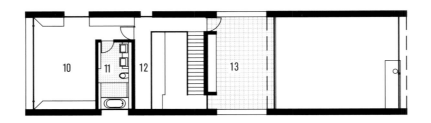

1 Driveway
2 Entry stair
3 Library
4 Bedroom 1
5 Bathroom
6 Laundry
7 Toilet
8 Kitchen
9 Living/dining room
10 Master bedroom
11 Ensuite
12 Office
13 Pool deck

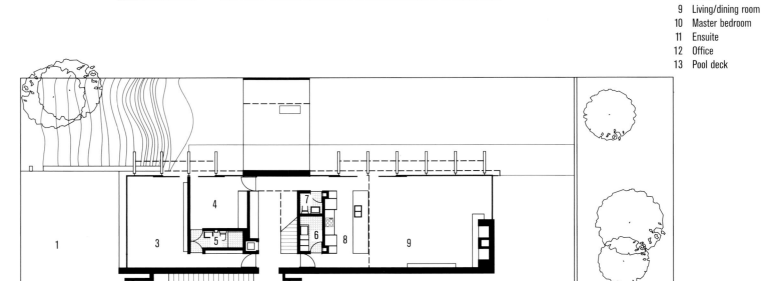

0   10m

This house is located in a cul-de-sac, on an elevated site

close to the city. When the architects first inspected the site, they realised the best vantage point was from the roof. 'The street really didn't say a lot. Many of the houses have high brick fences,' says architect Tim Black. 'We wanted not only to build a new home, but also to activate the street'. There is no high brick wall to the street, so neighbours can see into the front garden and view the activity within the house (at least into the library).

Known as the 'Wrap House', it takes its name from the idea of wrapping a material to create a house. 'The usual process is to work in a two-dimensional way, deciding where the rooms are going to be located and then creating the form,' says Black. However in this instance BKK was more interested in creating a modernist object that emerged from folding and manipulating one continuous plane.

Constructed of concrete blocks, rendered cement sheeting and floor-to-ceiling glass, the house is approached via a dramatic staircase that leads from the naturalist-style garden. The walls and roof of this entrance are made from a spray-painted metal deck and extend into the interior spaces. This compressed space leads to a light-filled, double-height void. To one side of this void is the library (front of the house) and to the other side the kitchen and family room. A bedroom and powder room separate the two spaces. The main bedroom, study and ensuite are upstairs, reached via the striking staircase.

The service elements (on both levels), located at the centre of the house, appear as self-contained units. 'Areas such as the kitchen could have emerged from the ground. They're almost the anchoring element,' says architect Simon Knott. The main living area, to the rear of the house, has a light and transparent feel and incorporates unusual elements such as a fireplace, made of rendered block work that appears to have been 'dragged' around the wall. Likewise, unusual lime-green joinery in the library simply winds its way around the wall.

Photography by John Gollings

index

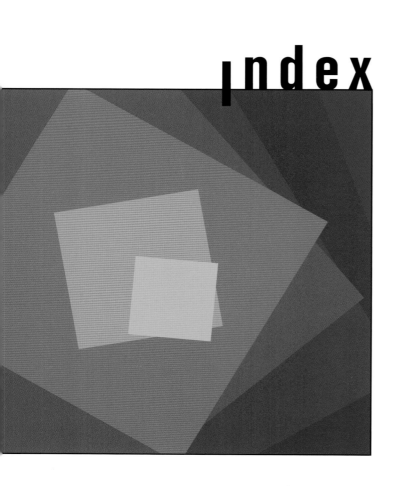

I would like to thank the architects featured in this book for pushing the boundaries and creating buildings that make us think about architecture and what it can achieve. Thanks must also go to the many photographers who contributed to this book, making the architect's vision that much stronger. I would especially like to thank my partner, Naomi, for her support, constructive comments and patience.

STEPHEN CRAFTI

Acknowledgments